Yu-Gi-Oh!

W9-BIE-996

JOEY WHEELER

the official character & monster guide

by arthur "sam" murakami

SCHOLASTIC INC

New York Toronto London Auckland Sydney
Mexico City New Delhi Hong Kong Buenos Aires

Cover design: Aruna Goldstein

Interior design: Rocco Melillo/Julia Sarno

ISBN: 0-7172-9915-5

12 11 10 9 8 7 6 5 4 3   6 7 8 9 10 11/0

Printed in the U.S.A.

First printing, May 2006

JOEY WHEELER

FROM BULLY TO BUDDY

Joey Wheeler was a hotheaded street kid who used to intimidate and harass the quiet kid at school—Yugi. Joey even stole a piece of Yugi's precious Millennium Puzzle so that Yugi couldn't complete it. However, Joey learned the error of his ways when Yugi protected Joey from the biggest bully in school. Joey and Yugi quickly became good friends. Though Joey could be quick to lose his temper, he had a kind heart and would do anything to back up his friends. Joey gave Yugi back the missing final piece of the Millennium Puzzle, and the rest is history.

FROM CHUMP TO CHAMP

Joey started out as a pretty-bad duelist and lost all the time. He couldn't even defeat Tea. When Yugi examined Joey's deck, all he found were tons of powerful monster cards. It's true that powerful monsters are important, but Joey didn't understand that he needed to mix spells and traps with his creatures to form cool combos. Luckily, Yugi taught him the fine points of dueling. Yugi's grandfather was willing to teach the young duelist a thing or two.

Joey's dueling style reflects his personality—his deck is full of risky cards where every play is a gamble. He uses many cards that rely on the flip of the coin or the toss of the dice, such as Time Wizard, Skull Dice and Graceful Dice. However, don't think that he only wins by luck—he has the skills to back it up. Don't forget—luck is a part of skill.

IT'S HARD BEING JOEY...

Joey did not have an easy life. Since Joey hadn't seen his sweet sister Serenity for years. The two lived apart. Serenity was losing her eyesight.

Yet there was hope. Doctors could cure Serenity's eye problems with an expensive operation. To help pay for the operation, Joey entered the Duelist Kingdom Tournament to win grand prize money. In addition, Joey wanted to help Yugi rescue his grandfather from the clutches of Pegasus.

THE ROAD OF A DUELIST

In his first-ever tournament duel, Joey faced off against Mai Valentine, one of the toughest duelists in the game. Mai had many victories under her belt. When Joey defeated Mai, he took the first halting step on the road to becoming a true duelist. Mai, who was always a loner, sensed something special about Joey, and a budding curiosity began that would bloom into a unique friendship.

The victory against Mai was only the beginning of Joey's crazy adventures in Duelist Kingdom: Joey won his signature monster, Red-Eyes B. Dragon, from Rex Raptor. Bandit Keith and his minions kidnapped Joey, forcing him to duel against Bonz in a creepy cave with his even creepier zombie monsters.

Although Joey was slowly losing his mind in these climatic clashes, his skills were gradually improving.

Yugi proved that Joey could more than hold his own when the two friends agreed to team up in a tag-team match against the Paradox Brothers, Pegasus' potent rhyme duelists. Since Yugi had far more experience than Joey, it was obvious that Joey was the weak link on the team. The Paradox Brothers used this knowledge to their advantage by targeting their attacks and strategies solely on Joey. However, Joey proved that he took a back seat to no duelist when he and Yugi combined their monsters to take down the brothers. Joey earned the right to enter Pegasus' castle for the Duelist Kingdom Finals.

FRIENDS AND FOES

In Joey's first battle of the Duelist Kingdom Finals, Joey was seeded to face Bandit Keith, the devious duelist who kidnapped Joey earlier in the tournament. Each duelist was required to have a special tournament entry card to participate in the finals. However, since Bandit Keith snuck into the tournament, he was the only finalist not to have the card. Therefore, the night before the finals, Bandit Keith stole Joey's entry card while Joey was asleep dreaming about doughnuts.

On the day of the duel, Joey discovered that his entry card was missing. He only had five minutes to find the card before he was disqualified. He retraced his steps and searched everywhere. Little did Joey know that Bandit Keith had the all-important card. Then, at the last possible moment, Mai unexpectedly gave her entry card to Joey. Joey had newfound respect for Mai, and he wasn't going to let this second chance go to waste. He took down Bandit Keith and his mechanical monsters by introducing Red-Eyes Black Metal Dragon. Joey clearly showed that cheating doesn't pay.

For the right to challenge Pegasus and win the prize money for Serenity's operation, Joey reluctantly had to square off against Yugi. Although they were the best of friends, Joey had to win if there was any chance of saving Serenity's eyesight. Despite Joey's new strategies and techniques that sent Yugi to the ropes, Yugi pulled out the victory in the end.

Joey was crushed. He lost his one chance to pay for Serenity's operation. Good friends are hard to come by, and Yugi was the best. Yugi gave the prize money to Joey so that he could pay for the surgery. Little did Joey know that Yugi's generous act would eventually come back and save Joey's life.

IT'S TIME FOR BATTLE CITY!

The next big competition was Kaiba's Battle City Tournament, an invitation-only contest among the world's top duelists. Kaiba was out to top Pegasus' Duelist Kingdom Tournament, and he was successful. Joey was psyched to compete, but trouble arose even before the tournament began.

The Rare Hunter, a devious duelist who steals rare cards from elite competitors, used Exodia the Forbidden One to obliterate Joey, and he took Joey's Red-Eyes B. Dragon. He had lost one of his strongest monsters, leaving Joey at a severe disadvantage. However, Joey proved that his skills had greatly improved by defeating many duelists, including Yugi's former adversaries Weevil and Mako, without the aid of Red-Eyes B. Dragon.

BRAINWASHED

Though Joey was on a winning streak, tragedy struck in the form of a sinister sneak. Marik, the evil leader of the Rare Hunters, disguised himself as the kind and gentle Namu, and befriended Joey in order to join his crew. When Marik got Joey alone, he used the magic of his Millennium Rod to brainwash and control Joey. Marik forced Joey to duel Yugi in a deadly duel where the loser was sent plummeting into the ocean with an anchor tied around his leg.

Marik knew that Yugi wouldn't allow Joey to drown, and he was right. Yugi sacrificed himself and allowed Joey to win, causing Yugi to sink into the depths of the sea. Fortunately, through Yugi's friendship and his bond with Red-Eyes B. Dragon, Joey broke out Marik's mind control. Joey quickly dived into the water and pulled Yugi to the surface. However, Joey used up all his strength to rescue Yugi, so he didn't have the energy to swim. Joey began to drown.

As Joey sank, he knew that his life was all over. He was about to give up when he saw someone diving towards him. It was his sister Serenity. Now that she could see from her successful eye operation, she was able to see Joey underwater and rescue him. After countless years, the Wheeler siblings were finally reunited.

FAILED PAYBACK

In the Battle City Finals, Marik defeated and trapped Mai's mind in the Shadow Realm, and Joey was determined to get her back. Joey wanted payback for everything Marik did: payback for hypnotizing him, forcing him to duel Yugi and almost end his life, and sending Mai's mind to the shadows.

In Joey's most terrifying Shadow Game ever, Marik's Egyptian God, The Winged Dragon of Ra, continued to blast Joey with searing heat and ferocious flames. The onslaught sapped Joey's strength. Despite massive injuries and tremendous pain, Joey kept fighting, refusing to give up.

Through sheer will and tenacity, Joey grabbed the advantage in the duel. All Joey had to do was summon one final monster to defeat Marik. Unfortunately, the enormous pressure of the Shadow Game, coupled with monumental physical and mental damage, caused Joey's stamina to run out. Joey collapsed before he could summon his monster, fell into unconsciousness, and lost the duel.

Asleep in the hospital, there was no sign that Joey would ever open his eyes again. However, deep in his dreams, Joey knew that Yugi would need his help to defeat Marik. Joey's bond with Yugi allowed him to regain his senses just in time to cheer Yugi on to victory!

A TRUE DUELIST

Days after the end of the Battle City Tournament, Dartz and his Grand Dragon Leviathan used the power of the sinister Orichalcos to wreak havoc on Earth, causing natural disasters to ravage the world. The Monster Realm called upon three true duelists to wield the power of the three Legendary Dragons and stop Dartz. If Joey still had questions on whether he was a true duelist or not, his questions were answered when the Legendary Dragon Hermos chose Joey to wield its power.

Joey's first battle against Dartz's minion was against Mai. Joey didn't know what to do. If he defeated Mai, her soul will be taken by the Orichalcos and sacrificed for Grand Dragon Leviathan's resurrection. However, if he lost to Mai, his soul would be taken, and he wouldn't be able to defeat Dartz. Fortunately, the duel ended in a draw, but this unfortunate reunion was far from over.

Joey and the gang traveled across the United States, battling Dartz's minions from coast to coast. Joey won the climactic battle against Dartz's loyal subject Valon. The battle was so devastating that Joey could barely see straight. Before Joey could catch his breath, he immediately had to duel against Mai. This time, the duel would not end in a draw.

Joey lost, and the Orichalcos took his soul. All that was left of Joey's body was a ravaged shell. However, Joey's sacrifice broke the spellbinding force that was overwhelming Mai. Joey reminded Mai that he would always be her friend and brought her back to the side of good.

Yugi rescued Joey's soul from Dartz, and they joined forces to finish off Dartz and his Grand Dragon Leviathan for the last time.

GREATEST CHALLENGE

With the world safe once again, it was time for Yugi and the Pharaoh to unlock the mysteries of ancient Egypt. Though the Pharaoh went back to the past alone, Yugi soon found out that the Pharaoh needed their help to stop an ancient menace from conquering the world. It was time for Joey to head back into the past to protect the present.

Though this might seem like Joey's biggest challenge, it was nothing compared to the real danger—he had to keep his eyes on Duke and Tristan because they both wanted to be Serenity's boyfriend.

JOEY'S MONSTER COLLECTION

RED-EYES B. DRAGON

CARD STATS

ATK::	2400
DEF::	2400
Level:	7
Attribute:	Dark
Type:	Dragon

Joey's favorite monster actually first belonged to Rex Raptor! Joey won it from the dino duelist at Duelist Kingdom, and good ol' Red-Eyes has stuck by his side ever since. That's a great thing because this ferocious dragon blasts inferno flames at its enemies and burns them to a crisp!

Before the Battle City Tournament, Joey had a horrible run-in with Marik's Rare Hunter. When Joey lost to the Rare Hunter's Exodia the Forbidden One, the Rare Hunter took Red-Eyes B. Dragon from him. Fortunately, Yugi defeated the Rare Hunter and got Red-Eyes B. Dragon back. However, when Yugi tried to give Red-Eyes B. Dragon back to Joey, Joey refused to take it until he felt his skills were worthy of his beloved dragon.

When Marik brainwashed Joey, Joey had to duel against Yugi where the loser would drown in the ocean. Yugi played Red-Eyes B. Dragon against Joey because he believed that Joey's bond with his most favorite monster could break Marik's spell. Joey felt his mind was tearing apart, but in the end, Yugi's friendship and his love for Red-Eyes B. Dragon defeated Marik's brainwashing.

During the Dartz saga, Red-Eyes went through some stunning transformations. Not only did it change into a stunning sword for Gearfried the Swordmaster, but Red-Eyes also morphed into a new form of armor that Joey could wear in his duel against Valon. Joey and Red-Eyes became one, literally.

CARD STATS

Level:	8
Attribute:	Dark
Type:	Machine

RED-EYES BLACK METAL DRAGON

Red-Eyes B. Dragon is extremely powerful, but when combined with the hardening properties of Metalmorph, it becomes Red-Eyes Black Metal Dragon. Joey used the metallic monster to take down Bandit Keith and his Barrel Dragon.

GEARFRIED THE IRON KNIGHT

The ferocious warrior Gearfried the Iron Knight is clad in extremely heavy armor, and there's a reason: Legend has it that Gearfried was so powerful that he couldn't contain his own strength. Therefore, he wore bulky armor to keep his power in check.

Gearfried is already very powerful as the Iron Knight, so what would happen if he took off his armor? Rex Raptor found out in the Dartz saga when Gearfried shed his armor, turning into Gearfried the Swordmaster. He unleashed his fury to slice Rex's dinosaurs into extinction.

CARD STATS

LEVEL:	4
ATTRIBUTE:	EARTH
TYPE:	WARRIOR

HERMOS

CARD STATS

ATK:	N/A
DEF:	N/A
Level:	N/A
Attribute:	N/A
Type:	N/A

Hermos was one of the three legendary dragons of the Monster Realm. When Dartz and the evil properties of the Orichalcos threatened to destroy Earth and the Monster Realm, he called upon Joey to stop the menace.

Hermos has the ability to combine with other monsters to form weird and wonderful new weapons. Joey first received Hermos' help in his duel against Mai at Industrial Illusions. Joey was one move away from losing the duel, but he joined Hermos with Time Wizard to form Time Magic Hammer— a terrific tool that pounded Joey's enemies into a time vortex and away from battle, giving Joey the opening to attack.

When Hermos joined with Red-Eyes B. Dragon, they transformed into a slaying sword that Gearfried the Swordmaster wielded on his way to victory against Rex Raptor.

In Joey's duel against Valon, Joey combined Hermos with the petite Rocket Warrior, but the resulting Rocket Hermos Cannon was far from petite. The blast from this armament demolished Valon's nearly invincible armor.

CARD STATS

Level:	8
Attribute:	Light
Type:	Warrior

GILFORD THE LIGHTNING

Once Gilford the Lightning enters the fray, all his enemies get a tingly feeling down their spines. Gilford raises his sword and blasts bolts of lightning to electrocute his enemies where they stand. Joey used Gilford the Lightning against Marik in the Battle City Finals and almost walked away with the victory, but Marik eventually won.

JINZO

Joey won Jinzo from Espa Roba during the Battle City Tournament due to the ante rule. This cybernetic menace not only emits a circular energy wave from his hands, but when he wears his Amplifier helmet, his energy skyrockets! Don't let Jinzo catch you off guard because this is one monster that you can't trap—he destroys all of them before they can trigger.

CARD STATS

LEVEL:	6
ATTRIBUTE:	DARK
TYPE:	MACHINE

CARD STATS

Level:	4
Attribute:	Earth
Type:	Beast-warrior

PANTHER WARRIOR

This ferocious feline attacks by pouncing on its enemies with its honed sword! Joey began using Panther Warrior during the Battle City Tournament, and it came to great use to take down Mako's almighty Fortress Whale.

FLAME SWORDSMAN

This searing swordsman has been with Joey since the very beginning at Duelist Kingdom. With a sword of scorching flames, he can slice and burn his opponents, especially Rex Raptor's dinosaurs who were weak against fire.

CARD STATS

LEVEL: 5
ATTRIBUTE: Fire
TYPE: Warrior

CARD STATS

Level:	4
Attribute:	Light
Type:	Warrior

ROCKET WARRIOR

This diminutive warrior may not look like much, but you better watch out when it tucks its arms in and transforms into a rocket. In its Invincible Mode, Rocket Warrior blasts itself at its enemies at supersonic speed.

SWORDSMAN OF LANDSTAR

This swordsman may look like a piece of jelly with a miniscule sword, but you better not take Swordsman of Landstar lightly. In fact, never take any creature with a sword lightly. He comes from a long line of other Landstar warriors, including the armament-wielding Rifleman of Landstar and the martial arts master Grappling Warrior of Landstar.

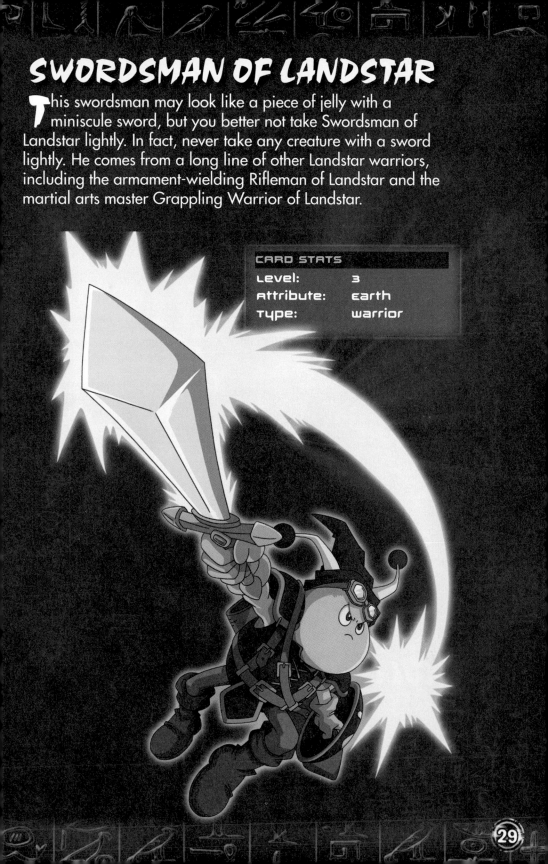

CARD STATS	
Level:	3
Attribute:	earth
Type:	warrior

CARD STATS

Level:	9
Attribute:	Dark
Type:	Dragon

B. SKULL DRAGON

Teaming up with Yugi always yields excellent results. Joey fused his Red-Eyes B. Dragon with Yugi's Summoned Skull to form a powerful dragon that shot molten fireballs and destroyed Paradox Brothers' nearly-invincible Gate Guardian.

DARK FLARE KNIGHT

Joey and Yugi are best buddies, and Dark Flare Knight proves it. Joey's Flame Swordsman fuses with Yugi's Dark Magician to form Dark Flare Knight, combining magic with swordplay. The Big Five's five-headed dragon didn't stand a chance against this warrior.

CARD STATS

Level: 6
Attribute: Dark
Type: Warrior

CARD STATS	
Level:	3
Attribute:	wind
Type:	dragon

BABY DRAGON

Never has a baby been so dangerous. Baby Dragon can breathe fire in your face and singe your eyebrows.

Baby Dragon is versatile. As he becomes older, he gains years of wisdom to become the smoke-spewing Thousand Dragon. He can also give a ride to Joey's Alligator Sword, transforming into the flying reptilian ravager Alligator's Sword Dragon. In the world of Capsule Monsters, Baby Dragon flew Joey to safety through a narrow canyon when he was chased by a flock of ferocious birds.

TIME WIZARD

What this wizard lacks in power, he more than makes up for in powerful time spells. By manipulating space and time, Time Wizard can summon portals to send enemies plunging into a time warp. He once used Time Magic to change Red-Eyes B. Dragon into a fossil that crumbled into dust. If you're not careful, Time Wizard won't send your enemies into a time warp—He'll send YOU into one.

CARD STATS	
Level:	2
Attribute:	Light
Type:	Spellcaster

CARD STATS

Level:	7
Attribute:	Wind
Type:	Dragon

THOUSAND DRAGON

With the help of Time Wizard, Baby Dragon ages a thousand years and gains a millennium's worth of knowledge to become the wise Thousand Dragon. Don't just be wary of its sharp claws—this dangerous dragon also has a ferocious nostril gust.

ALLIGATOR'S SWORD

CARD STATS

Level: 4
Attribute: Earth
Type: Beast

CARD STATS

Level: 5
Attribute: Wind
Type: Dragon

ALLIGATOR'S SWORD DRAGON

Alligator's Sword is a wyvern warrior who knows how to strike and parry against the best knights in the world. When he jumps on top of Baby Dragon to fuse into Alligator's Sword Dragon, he gains the power of flight and flames. Joey used Alligator's Sword Dragon to take on Mako during the Battle City Tournament and soared off into victory.

CARD STATS

Level:	5
Attribute:	earth
Type:	warrior

SWAMP BATTLEGUARD

Tristan and Joey may argue a lot, but they prove that they're good friends when their Swamp Battleguard and Lava Battleguard fight together.

You don't want to face two angry brothers, especially when they're wielding powerful clubs.

TIGER AXE

The name of this monster is self-explanatory: it's a terrorizing tiger with an awesome axe.

CARD STATS

Level:	4
Attribute:	earth
Type:	beast-warrior

AXE RAIDER

Showing no mercy, this monster strikes down his foes with abandon.

CARD STATS

Level:	4
Attribute:	earth
Type:	warrior

CARD STATS

Level:	3
Attribute:	Earth
Type:	Warrior

BATTLE WARRIOR

With a powerful punch, this monster KOs all his foes. Joey used Battle Warrior to deal the final blow against Bonz's zombies and send them back to the grave.

GAROOZIS

With twin scythes on its arms, it is ready to slash its way to victory.

BATTLE STEER

This battling bovine is very unique because it's one of the few monsters that wields a trident.

CARD STATS

Level: 5
Attribute: earth
Type: Beast-warrior

MEMORABLE DUELS

Joey's first victory:
Joey vs mai valentine—
Duelist Kingdom Tournament

Not only was this Joey's first duel in a major tournament, but Mai was as strong as she was beautiful, meaning she's one of the toughest duelists in the world. Mai further psyched out Joey because she had the uncanny ability to know what card she was drawing from her deck without even looking at it. She was psychic!

However, Joey used something he wasn't accustomed to using—his brains. He closed his eyes and was able to smell different scents. He figured out that Mai was putting various perfumes on the cards so that she could tell what card she drew by smell.

Though Joey solved Mai's trick, Mai was more than just theatrics. She had incredible skills to back it up. With her Harpie Lady Sisters, she clawed through Joey's monsters and punished him thoroughly. However, Joey turned the tables by using Time Wizard—which Yugi gave him as a gift—to age his Baby Dragon into the wizened Thousand Dragon while simultaneously transforming the Harpie Lady Sisters into ragged old women.

Joey's most embarrassing duel:
Joey vs Duke Devlin

Duke Devlin humiliated Joey in school with a parlor trick, making Joey look like a complete idiot. Joey wanted to prove who was boss by beating him in a duel. Joey didn't realize that Duke Devlin was an expert gamer who even invented the Dungeon Dice Monsters board game. Duke Devlin soundly defeated Joey, and as penalty for losing, Joey had to dress up like a dog and bark.

Joey's monsters are an eclectic bunch, but they all have one thing in common: Their attacks and abilities are

Monster	Attacks/Special Abilities
Axe Raider	Wind Blades
Battle Warrior	Ultimate Battle Fist
B. Skull Dragon	Molten Fireballs/ Claws of Flame
Blue Flame Swordsman	Dragon Sword Swipe
Flame Swordsman	Flaming Sword of Battle/Salamandra Flamestrike
Garoozis	Five-Slash Strike/ Battle Axe Crush
Gator Dragons	Wamp Fire Blast
Gearfried the Iron Knight	Metal Forearm Thrust
Gilford the Lightning	Lightning Sword

some of the most powerful in the game! Check out the names of their attacks and abilities!

Monster	Attacks/Special Abilities
Giltia the D. Knight	Soul Spear Assault
Jinzo	Psychic Wave/Cyber Energy Shock Lightning Fist Attack
Panther Warrior	Swift Panther Slash
Red-Eyes B. Dragon	Inferno Fire Blast
Red-Eyes Black Metal Dragon	Flash Flare Blast
Rocket Warrior	Invincible Attack
The Fiend Megacyber	Cyber Swipe
Thousand Dragon	Inferno Flame Breath/ Noxious Nostril Gust Noxious Vapor Gust
Time Wizard	Time Magic/ Time Roulette

JOEY'S FRIENDS

YUGI MUTO

Yugi is Joey's best friend. The great duelist taught Joey various strategies to improve his abilities. Now they are both highly skilled, and often help each other when the battles are tough.

TRISTAN TAYLOR

Joey and Tristan always insult and crack jokes on each other, but that's because they're such great buddies. Though Tristan often acts like a goofball, there's no one better than Tristan to have in your corner during a fight.

TÉA GARDNER

Tea is always there to root for Joey and the rest of the crew. As the cheerleader of the group, she helps keep Joey's spirits up when the chips are down.

SERENITY WHEELER

Her sweetness and timidity belies her innate courage. Who could forget that heroic moment when Serenity saved her drowning brother?

JOEY'S RIVALS

SETO KAIBA

Kaiba has many nicknames for Joey —and they're all unflattering: "Dueling Monkey," "Dog," and "Loser" are some of the nicer names. Kaiba doesn't think Joey has any skills whatsoever and is always the first to point that out. It also doesn't help Joey's reputation that Kaiba defeated him in both Duelist Kingdom and Battle City.

MARIK ISHTAR

Marik and his Rare Hunters stole his Red-Eyes B. Dragon, brainwashed him, made him battle in a deadly duel against Yugi, sent Mai to the Shadow Realm, and knocked him unconscious. Is there any argument why Joey doesn't like him?

DID YOU KNOW...

...that Joey was originally not allowed to enter Pegasus' Duelist Kingdom Tournament? Joey didn't have any Star Chips which were required to enter the tourney! However, Yugi shared his Star Chips with him, and Joey was allowed to enter!

...that Joey wasn't originally allowed to enter Kaiba's Battle City Tournament either? Kaiba said he wasn't skilled enough!

...that while Yugi defeated Weevil's Great Moth, Joey defeated Perfectly Ultimate Great Moth? Joey faced a more powerful version than the one Yugi had to face and passed with flying colors!

...that Joey lost to Tea in a duel? Joey was only a beginner, but he lost to her when his Rock Ogre Grotto #1 was turned to dust by Breath of Light.

...that though Joey lost to Zigfried in the KaibaCorp Grand Championship, he still did better than Weevil and Rex Raptor. Weevil and Rex Raptor lost to Zigfried in one turn!